This Is Not A Love Story

A Collection Of Poems

AUTHOR
CHAUNTAE MARABLE

Synopsis

I've never chosen a lover, I've always allowed myself to be chosen. This is not a love story as the title states but this is a story about the love that I've experienced over the years. As with any relationship there will be ups and downs. How you navigate those instances is what will determine how you'll love another as well as how you'll heal. I've spent countless years writing these words and finally my baby is being born. This is one woman's journey through pain, love, lust, heartache, confusion … see where I'm going with this? Lol ! I hope that these words and affirmations offer a path to healing for you as it has done with me. Going forward I put all of these thoughts of not being good enough and waiting to be chosen behind me as I embrace loving myself. I hope this book allows you a reflection of yourself or someone you know and we can all begin the process of healing

Table Of Contents

Talk Yo'Shit
I Want You To Fuck Me (Extended Session)
Ego
When I Tell You I Love You
Balance
Stubborn
Double Penetration
The End

Dedication

I dedicate this book to all of the resilient. The ones who pack up emotions like a suitcase and keep pressing on. The ones who have said 'I see their potential' only for their intended to end up elsewhere. Dedicated to the fixer uppers, the clean up women, the fed up women and the women who only know how to love hard.

This one is for us because I know what it feels like to desperately love someone and be unsure of their intentions towards you.

My tribe … damn y'all!! I thank you for the advice, the eye rolls, the shoulders to cry on, the movie dates to cheer me up and overall the conversations we've been able to have to get me to this point. Antares Nikki Davinci, you have been so supportive through this entire journey.

Thank you for sharing your experiences with me and your advice. Nadirah, sisssss we give em back to the streets … period! Thank you for everything that you do. Erica, since 1995 we have been ride or die! I'm glad we've grown out of our wild ways but I know we can still get it poppin if need be. To Jess and Squishy I love y'all dynamic. Thank you for allowing me to vent and understanding that I needed to be loved through my mistakes.

To my lovers … the way you hurt me inspired me. I thank you for the pain and the lessons.

To anyone reading this book I thank you for taking a chance on me, for the opportunity to be vulnerable with you and for the journey as you flip the pages.

Grab your wine or favorite brown and get comfy. This ain't a love story, but it's a damn good poem book

- Chauntae

I'm always Too Much until they find themselves
with a bunch of Not Enoughs

This Is NOT A LOVE STORY

Copyright 2020

Playlist Selection

A good book accompanied by a good playlist will elevate the experience.
I have created a playlist for this book.
I hope these songs transport you back to a place when you were happy.

Moods & Music, a playlist by lilmissmessy on Spotify

Moods & Music

Mood Enhancements

Supplied by: IG: Rosebutterbodyco
www.rosebutterbodyco.com

"Get Your Mind Right Meditation Kit"

Volume I - Miss Not Your Type

This is not a love story as I've never
picked a lover
I've always allowed myself to be chosen
I allowed myself to receive
Unwatered love

Visions

You provide the music as I set the mood

My hips undulate against the sheets as your tongue begins its melody

A journey against brown skin

Glowing

Hot

Scented essence from its core

A beat fitting better than your favorite pair of jeans

This mood has to be created, the love leaves me elated

"If i would have known the girl next door would have been you"

This meeting of mind & soul would have happened much sooner

Open your eyes to not your selfish desire and wants, but to the desires of others.

Give pleasure by giving all of you

Complete the circle, a bond never to be broken

Vows to make you happy leading to moments of reflection Love, with cherubic faces

and brown eyes we get lost in

Swim in my gene pool, the sensation will leave you gasping for air.

Play Me A Snippet

~So I know this love is real
~So I know the exchange will be mentally satisfying
~So I know I will be hopelessly in love

Play me a snippet of our love

Fast forward to the part after the day you left then slow it down so i can catch my breath…
speed it up past this part, I love when you come to me.
You touch my heart, every part of me beats.
 My toes that quicken my steps, the lingering on my lips after the brief kiss, a snippet of my life

A snippet of what it may be like to be your wife. I know we just met and this may be too deep but how many lovers would you have bypassed with a blessed sneak peak?

I need a double feature with an unlimited amount of sequels. Damn, i just want a snippet of your love… even if it's just the preview.

You expect me to go on faith alone? You said it's good, well I've heard that too many times and most of those movies only got played once. I know that in love there are no guarantees, however, my sorrows and wants need a greater purpose for my heart.

Nothing worse than getting caught up in a good film only to dislike the ending. Don't be afraid to give me the uncut. I need to base my desires on more than just luck.

Equate you to a bootlegger. Very affordable for my heart, thinking I can buy love with dimples and an ass of notable size. I need a documentary but I want a snippet 1st.

Woman who I desire, please play me a snippet of our love

You're So Arrogant

I'm so caught up
Can't regret that I fell in love, I'm so in love with love
Your eyes that always wander
That smile reserved for someone else
The light touch your share recklessly
I'm in love so these things get overlooked
Hmmmm, if she walked a mile in my shoes…
Well shit...she'd be a mile ahead and not hopelessly in love

- *If someone wants to be in your life they will be there. They do not have to be forced or swayed. Love is what binds two people, no matter what. Forgiveness prevents future or past behaviors from destroying your heart - Chauntae*

Humility

My apologies aren't good enough for you - you haven't even began to apologize to me for all your missteps

These transgressions I overlook due to love.

You threaten me with your presence. I am no longer scared to be alone. Conceding in an argument was a part of my growth so everytime you challenge me, I win.

I will not excuse my emotion or be tolerant of yours

That fine line you say I dance on is now held together by me

No longer am I balancing on your strings

The benefit of you is for my heart.

My heart is pure for you but your actions and words make me question the static in my brain.

Trying to be heard when someone won't listen is a harrowing task.

Always playing the defensive because you use your size against me… I don't like that

I know i'm broken and I need fixing, try opening those pretty brown eyes

For the safety of my heart we can never be more than just friends. The emotion you pull is detrimental to my health

Bigger Picture

Lying in wait while you're lying, I'll wait

Are you tired of trying?

I'm tired of arguing

Getting nowhere in our years, too spent to shed tears. Emotional rollercoaster and i'm begging to get off

I let it be your decision, you rode the ride now get off

Focused on you so long my reflection is a blur

Focused on making me better so I'd get the treatment you gave her

Refuse to claim titles when I know my worth

My big picture includes a ring and I know its worth

Not looking for you to fulfill a need you can't

I shouldn't have put that responsibility on you, apparently that role is too advanced

You'd rather shrink than grow but baby, I water all seeds

Just remember I'm no longer here when you figure out I'm the one that you need

Back of your throat

Run your tongue over my love and let it hit the back of your throat.

This shit I kick with no touch involved is what makes it no joke.

Have you ever had a pussy you never had?

A mental fuck from me and you'll be glad

Simple conversation with sexual innuendo is all I'm praying for.

Stick those lips against my ears and watch me visibly drip

Verbal manifestations cause my chest to heave and my pussy to pop

Bend me over with each verse and you better fuck me hard

Pound these words in and out, i'm fucking you now

Run your tongue over my love and let it hit the back of your throat

Good Bye My Love

It seems that I was right.
A temporary fixture designed for your healing before you book flight.
I guess I can't be too surprised.
I would have seen it if not for my reluctance to look you in your eyes.
So much time wasted, so much love abated.
Always thought it was good to love you more than I loved me, guess I was wrong again.
Look where it left me.
Exactly 12 tears fell tonight. I promise that's all I'll waste.
I wonder if I never called would my heart still break.
If i'd stayed home instead of meeting you for our 1st date… all the signs said I should run

I allowed you to make me your toy.
I hope it was fun. Release yourself from me.
 Please. Don't. Come. Back.

There is no way to fix this. The stage is black.

Entertained the thought of being so much more to you but always ended up so much less to you. How do you not love me?

The realist shit I ever heard was that you can't raise a grown ass person. People only change if they want to. I wanted to change for you… for us.

I hope you regret meeting me.

I hope you forget how much you thought you loved me.

I hope you forget the measure I set and the bar I raised.
I hope they make you happy.

You will never have love like I tried to give it to you.

I'm not even mad, I'm just disappointed in myself. I could have found the love of my life by now but i was fucking around with you.

Maybe it was one of the many I turned away.

Damn, I should have fucked them all

Imprint

I've had my eyes on you for quite some time. Always wanted to spend just a little time.

When I left you I touched myself.

Rolling in my bed covered in your scent. Fingers squeezing, rubbing, moaning, wanting to fill this deep longing inside of me.

I want you to fuck me, only, im not sure you can handle me properly.

Your touch was innocent, hesitant is what i'll say… we both agree i'm more aggressive than you.

Your scent is intoxicating and your demeanor is just the same. I could drink you daily. I'm seasoned and a predator some would say. You call me cocky and I like that shit.

I'd love to taste your thoughts and swallow your inhibitions.

Insert two fingers inside your deep emotions and rub your frustrations across my lips.

Imprinting on you to make you mine.

I've already ruined you, unaware you were caught in the trap

Miss Not Your Type

Tired of the nice girl rap, invented the zone of friends where I get placed after you've experienced and decided that I wasn't your taste.

Your homie, lover, friend, taking 'love her' out of the equation… not your type but good enough to fuck

Miss independent, but you want a bitch who's needy.
I'm giving my time and money but my body is greedy.
I crave the closeness of being a unit with you. I'm asking for sex, thats not enough for me to fall in love with you.
I have been called a remarkable woman yet, single is where I reside

Working on being everything you don't know you want, watching our inner struggle of feelings of wanting, lust and desire.
I'm tired of being Miss Not Your Type.
I refuse to try harder.
Your perception of the perfect woman will leave you heartbroken every time.
I never should have let you
I knew what I was doing when I pursued you.
 I just didn't know the chain of events would cause such a drastic reaction.
Shit you had bitches, I had bitches too
You were supposed to be SAFE
I'm Miss Not Your Type right?
Miss no feelings, fuck em, duck em, leave em and all that shit right?
I knew I was in trouble the 1st time I tasted you
Preying on your weakness I opened what little was left of your heart and demanded entry for my selfish desires
I wanted you
Purely for carnal pleasure
The rest was shit that got in the way
A situation turned into a situation, turned into a break up and we was just supposed to be fucking but you saw my future intent and ran, I could have chased you, but the me in me said fuck it, you'll miss me.
Problem is, I miss you too
So much about you i never knew
Much more than a pretty face, your insecurities make you sexy
Your wonder gives me hope that i'm not broken and …
Oh fuck this!
I never should have let you let me in

Don't fall in love with girls like me
We are trouble because we will tell you the truth
I let you see my truth and you are scared of the love I could give you
They all were…
unselfish with love and I want to give it all to you baby
But I can't
I'm Miss Not Your Type
waiting in the shadows
Watching you make stupid mistakes in love
Crazy thing is…
I never wanted to be your girl

Needy

I love to see you smile, nothing like putting it there myself

I could stare at you all day

Pretty baby you are however, much more than a beautiful face and far from a child

You intrigue me and I can't leave you alone

Our scents mingle to make the perfect fragrance and I want to bottle us up so I never run out of the memory

I see the pain and struggle behind those pretty brown eyes, watching you hurt causes me pain

You need me to love you and I need someone … no, I need to love you too

Mine

She kissed me and I backed away selfishly wanting her taste on my lips to myself.

I rubbed the outline of her lips and whispered...Mine

I wasn't looking for anything you put in my path.

Convinced I was ok, fine, unbothered and whatever other adjectives come to mind.

Me... a loner by choice. I choose to stay out of the social scene.

Attracted, but indifferent

Timing

It's everything

Soul Mates

Purposeful Living

Waiting Game

Marriage

Commitment

Devotion

Just be into me

She tells me my time is coming. I have to be patient

She tells me my time is coming, I have to be patient

A beautiful distraction, all talk, less interaction.

So used to loving all the wrong ones

Her against Me

Damn, I said I wanted something different and again I forgot that I speak with intention.

I was looking for love just not right now.

You held a mirror to my facade and forced me to be who I am. Prejudged you and I fucked that all up.

Thought I could convince you I wasn't what you wanted and turns out you like broken things

Damn, I guess you can put me back together. Scared to take on the pain you don't know needs releasing.

Scared to be vulnerable, to give my all… would you take my pieces and hold them close to your heart

A love like ours, more than physical contact. Innocent and intense.

Letting go of fears can have a beautiful reward

A Wife

Haven't thought of myself in that role in years. It's crazy I can see it with you.

I tell myself this is exactly how it starts with them all.

I roll my eyes and prepare myself for the fall or the let down because I know you're too good to be true.

What exactly did I do to deserve you?

What are you doing to deserve me?

I wasted her time, and I might have wasted yours too.

As I am you want me...fuck... that wasn't how this game was played.

Last Night

Wet
Taste
Soft
Intimate
Comfort

Pain

Take all your frustrations on me. Allow me to soothe you with the rhythm of my hips. Allow my hands to caress your demons. Release them onto me.

Suck out good intentions and bask in light and love. Transference of energy is handled well on my end. I overflow with praise, kneel at my altar. Sex with me is amazing. You'll change, you'll crave

Lay your head on my chest, relax, unwind, heal. You need this last night to placate your demons. Let me in one last night.

Let me be perfect in your eyes only. Breathing in sync, bodies intertwined, intimacy displaced

You aren't ready for another night like that.

I can give you a facade… although we are good together

Last night was the end

Woman with Strings

Out of my element you pull emotion I don't want to explore

I tell you I'm fine yet you see through me and caress the worry from my lips with your tongue

Not caring about anyone else

Time not allowing anyone in my space

You infiltrated my entire being.

I suffocate without you.

Loving is not challenging yet loving you has been my greatest challenge

So close to giving up what's the use of forcing something you clearly don't want, are clearly resistant to

Why are you here

Is it to torment me with the possibility of what if? Something that will never be more than what it is?

Is this what you do Woman with Strings?

Are these your past lovers hanging like leaves refusing to fall to the ground?

The foundation may be strong but the weight of your tree leaves little room to build.

Does your tree not shed as the seasons intend? Although there is beauty to be seen I'd like to see your branches.

I need you bare, woman with strings. I need your leaves to fall so I can properly water your roots.

Trim your tree to make room for me

Love

Is it ever enough?
Is it ever truthful?
Is it ever meant to be?
Is it even for me?

I wear my emotions like tattered clothes grazing my skin. An eyesore for sure because I relish in their comfort.

I don't mind the lies or the smiles that never quite reach your eyes. I don't need your love, especially when it comes with… complications

You'd do anything to keep me but tell me the truth to keep me.

You pretend I'm important when in reality a convenience is more like it.

Knowing and doubting my worth at the same time, too old, too damn fine to be caught up in your web, in your bed, you reside in my head.

Decision making I don't trust. I love you and you broke that for lust. Trying to break free but you won't let me go… Let me go

You confuse me. I'm not used to… wait, I know this pattern and I know what happens, torn between two. What we have dissipates unbeknownst to you.

No more smiles or words of endearment. No I love you's or affection, lack of attention due to your indiscretion. Mood swings, shifty beings, spirit unaligned, too much pride and truth to deny.

Refuse to share or if i do I'll never care. You become a toy, a playmate, a series of dates… let me go, there's no need for me to be here.

Lovers with an unfinished past. After learning your truth I wish I'd never seen you laugh. Wish I was never drawn to that smile. Wish I never opened my mouth to say hi. Wish you would have told me the truth. The importance of her, exactly who she is to you.

Love should have been enough… at least for you to choose me

She said

I can't lose you

    -What are you doing to keep me? Especially with how you choose to treat me

She said: Baby i'm sorry

    -Sorry you got caught. Cant make up for the hurt no matter how many gifts you bought

She said: I know I fucked up

    -You knew it at the time. I'm supposed to stay knowing you shared what was supposed to be mine?

She said: We can fix this

    -We didn't break it. I don't desire to be a part of your construction.

She said: Let's rebuild our trust

    -Never trust a woman you hurt

She said: You know you have my heart

    -You don't even have your heart. Are you willing to take it from her to give it to me?

She said: Why do you always gotta start?

    -I don't, let's finish.

Unspoken words include, Be happy, just go with the flow. Don't let the hurt consume you, eventually she'll know.

Keep waiting to be chosen.

Wondering what she's doing at night.

Elevated breathing anytime her phone rings or chimes.

Keep giving yourself anxiety.

When she chooses you then what?

Do you trust her?

Should she trust you?

Are you really going to make this work?

I want you to fuck me

I've been thinking of you fucking me. Lick me all over my body and suck on me. Remember that time when we fucked on the couch? Desire spilled over when I put you in my mouth. Baby my pussys been wet since you left me this morning.

Can you fuck me on the counter and then on the floor? Wait baby, don't stop, go deeper, give me more. Throw them legs back, way back how you like. Beat this pussy up baby. You fuck me just right.

Ooohhhh mhmm yeah baby right there. You want me to bend over? I love when you whisper that nasty shit in my ear. Dripping, squirting, oozing, gushing wet and overflowed.

Pulling you close letting you know that this is your pussy. Scratching and biting, strokes getting deeper, eyes locked on mine so enticing.

Licking the side of your neck tasting the work you put in. Deeper, harder, slower, I feel my release coming, put it back in

I want you to fuck me just like this every time. Fuck me like you believe it when you ask is it mine.

Fucking up the sheets, they really didn't stand a chance. Damn I love them back shots smacking and gripping my ass.

You touch me just right, my body surrenders to you. Baby... I can't even finish. That's how bad I want to fuck you.

I never knew

Sometimes I wonder just how long you had your eye on me. Of course i'll never know but it's fun to ponder the mystery.

Across a dimly lit room you watched continuously...watching, waiting, smiling, planning?

Why not approach me, maybe take a chance. May not have given you my number but surely a dance. I wonder why you waited, then appeared out of the blue.

Was it because you were afraid I finally noticed you? I never knew

Tell Her

Tell her I can feel her energy

I can smell her as soon as she walks into a room

In a crowd full of people it is just she and I

Our movements coincide, hearts beating rapidly

No words needed, every touch perfectly harmonized

Her voice is a caress, even the way she blinks turns me on

Tell her i watch her with eyes shut, tell her the fluidity of her movements haunt my dreams

Her aura is peaceful. To bask in her glow gives me a calm i've never felt

Tell her im in love before i know her name

Tell her, because i've never seen her

The Artist

My body wears your name, they could find it if they knew where to look

I feel your caress with every step that I take

Longing for you, a taste only you can satisfy. No longer content, no longer content imagining you here.

Need turns into desperation as I frantically rub my legs together to stop the fire beginning to burn

I've made my decision. I Want You

I want to give you all of me, my treasured possessions, by unbridled passions

Playing like a movie in my head I see every move you make

You move to stroke I move to recieve
I take your stroke, you aim to please

Your touch elicits a keen response

My body unprepared for the sensations I now feel

Factor in the Ex

Lauren said, you let go and I'll let go too...

Very important words for her to speak cause when it comes to relationships and connections there's always a little bit of lingering emotion for the one who wasn't chosen

The one who wasn't chosen always feels as though they need to get back, they need to make a pact, they need to show their previous lover what they are missing in fact

If you continue to sit at this table you will starve because I refuse to feed you the love I pour from my heart

You won't eat off my plate, you won't eat from the meal I provide for her and I wont allow her to feed you scraps

What I have reserved for her is for her, now

I dropped into the middle of your love affair, unknowing, unassuming and i'm unwilling to let her go

If you both were in the right place, right space, right time ... I don't understand why you let her go.

I'm not understanding why you didn't commit to her.

I'm not understanding why the promises you made you didn't fulfill with her

I'm not understanding why you're mad at me for seeing the real in her

I'm not understanding why your mad at her for seeing me after what I saw in her

She's a phenomenal woman, she's made just for me, she's perfect in every way for me

I don't need her to change... she's exactly what and who i need her to be

She awakened a love in me that i thought i had buried long ago

She gets the best part of me and i get the best part of her

It could all be so simple.. But you'd rather make it hard

I don't expect you to disappear into thin air but until our foundation is strong i need you to not be there

Only popping up when you realize the attention is no longer there

Giving just enough of yourself so that she believes you care
I see through that shit and will extend my vision to her

I plan to marry this woman, do you think you are going to interfere with that?

I plan to love this woman, do you think after the way I love she'll ever want you back?

I'm planning a future with this woman that doesn't include your love

Consider yourself uninvited and leave the table before you get a shove

Battleground

I doubted my ability to continue to love you
How is it I woke up today more in love with you than ever before
Through all of the pain, through all of the tears, through all of the everything
I'm still able to see the light that shines within you
My mind and my heart are in constant battle
I know this is fucked up, I know I should give up, I know I should leave you, I know that
shit is rough, I know I should do what everyone else has done to you
But my heart is telling me stay
My heart is telling me that you'll provide a way
My heart is telling me you'll meet me halfway
My heart is telling me that we are connected
My heart is telling me that you won't leave
My heart is telling me that i should stay
My heart is telling me that you are the other piece
You are my peace
When i'm around you I find my smile
When you need a smile I can bring it to you
Soul mate, karmic connection, twin flame
All of that shit, it applies but it's not us
We have our own shit going on
Not even supposed to be what we are, but what we are is meant to be
It's very simple
I love you
It's even simpler
You love me
Fighting for each other has never been a problem
We are under attack, we have to fight together, not apart

Walk away from love

I've never been in a position where I had to make a decision where I wasn't sure if it was the right decision for me

How do you walk away from someone you love when you're still in love with them

How do you claim to be in love with someone when you can't even say that you love them

How do you allow the pain to engulf you so completely that it turns you dark

Void of all emotion, I still want you

Void of all emotion the desire is still present

Do you realize I have to re-learn how to love you
The version of you that I loved was a false pretense
I have to love the real you
I don't even know if I fucking like the real you

It's very easy for people to say you need to love yourself more
You need to put yourself first, you don't have to take that
You deserve better

It's easy to say that from the outside looking in
When your heart is involved and you feel that love shit deep in your soul
You feel like this is what you deserve because it makes you feel good
You feel like this is what you were searching for because it eases you it soothes you
You feel like you don't want to let this go
So you're willing to hold on to it at any cost

At what cost though?

Your sanity?
Your peace of mind?
Your healing?

Are you really ready to backtrack? Are you really ready to go through the healing process again for a situation you know doesn't serve you?

You woke up and all of a sudden she no longer fed you. Or were you just not hungry for the food she provided

You woke up and all of a sudden she didn't look the same

You woke up and all of a sudden you realized as long as you continue to allow her to do these things, she will continue to do these things because you are continuing to allow her

The both of you are

Loving you is like a battle and we both end up with scars… I'm tired of nursing my wounds. I'm tired of being on the battlefield with you.

Love is not war… not for me

Love is peace
Love is calm
Love is Energy

You've drained me dry…I don't have any love left in me

Expectations

I can show you love, embody love, be the one to love you unconditionally and wholeheartedly.

The moment i fell in love with you I felt that shit all through me and it pissed me the fuck off!

This wasn't supposed to happen, I mean I have no problem showing I care but I promised myself I would not fall, I promised myself I wouldn't lose myself in another soul.

The problem is I don't feel lost, I feel found if that makes sense. I feel like you could be that one and it's terrifying.

I'm doubting my ability to live up to the expectations you may have of me.

I don't want to fall short of the woman I know I am and the woman you inspire me to be.
I

don't want to love and give my all to something that isn't' reciprocal.

I love you.. But I want more out of this and I'm not sure where you stand. My foundation is solid and yours feels like sand. I'm unsteady, uneasy, unknowing, under a fog of your pseudo love.

What the fuck is this?

What the fuck are we because at this point I could be somewhere doing othere things.

I chose to give you my focus, choose to love you completely...for what?

A not ready?
For what?
Someone better?

I'll tell you like i told the last miserable bitch who thought she was better off without me... good luck with your clone.

Throwback Thursday

Take me back to the Thursday when you first told me you loved me

A time where love conquers all and pink and yellows fill our days because we only embrace happy over here

It's always good in the beginning… that first Thursday after the first time you met. When the smile still reaches your eyes...

Shadow Lover

Wild and untamed, the beauty of you starts at the top and filters down. Your hair is electricity personified. Free... I love when I touch with intention. Baby if I could I'd pour all my good into you just to be able to see it walking and talking I swear I would.

Your face coupled with your brown skin is a love song. The contours of you draw me in. Forehead, left cheek, right cheek, nose then chin ... pay attention to my kisses

The angle of your neck is perfect for the comfort it gives. The ability to lay in your presence and be still ... I'm always on the go and you make me comfortable enough to pause.

Shoulders, arms, back strong and soft and I love the way you feel. I love the way your muscles contract when I hug you, when I kiss you, when you fucked me. Poetry that I wish I could write all over your body. Every time I touch you a new word is formed you don't even see.

I can't say you've been hurt because you don't give in to that energy. I can say you haven't been worshiped... I'm not sure you've been desired... I can tell you I can do all those things but what are words without actions?

I'm going to tell you you are beautiful and I want you to feel that shit every time. I want it to attack your subconscious and pull that smile out of you. I want you to carry that shit throughout the day. Know that I mean it and your beauty comes from within... When I tell you that I think you're beautiful, know that I'm desiring you at that moment.

We

Baby we can fuck under the glow of a full moon as I read you my poetry.

Fill me with your words, coated in honey from your sweet lips. I wish for

you to devour me. I daydream of your mouth on my body taking what is

yours

Cause & Cure

Baby, you hurt me just to soothe me. Your words have deep meaning until they turn back into words.

The duality of you is unsettling and I can't grasp the way you love me. I'm used to giving my all... I told you you're not at 100% and instead of getting there your battery with me is slowly dying.

I know you think you're trying... shit I'm trying not to lose it. You already blew it. I'm here still because I care because I wonder if I wasn't who would be there?

Do they listen to your fears or even know what they are?

Slick tongue you have loving me near and them from afar.
Do they care about your well being?

Make sure you have food to eat? I'd sacrifice my last for you, heart wouldn't skip a beat.

Will they love you unconditionally? Despite all your flaws?

Have they gotten to know you, down to your preference in drawers? I've studied you, learned you, loved you, tolerated the disrespect.

You're my cause and my cure why haven't I left you yet?

I see so much in your future and mine. I know we are the perfect melody, it's just now isn't the time.

You spoon feed me dreams knowing what I desire. Yet as soon as I'm not around to turn to the one you desire.

It must be my karma for the hurt that I've caused.

Loving you or loving in general seems to be my biggest flaw. I give so much of me for so little in return, I drop so many tears my eyes begin to burn, no malice in my heart, losing me will fuck you up.

My cause and my cure ... I need to give this addiction up.

How to hurt me

What a powerful concept that leads to questions. No one ever asks how they can hurt you.

They ask how they can love you, how they can be there for you, how they can be acquainted.

I like to answer questions that haven't been asked. Here's how to hurt me...

Listen to my fears and tell me you'll be there

Absorb my love and tell me you love me

Hear my truth and lie to me profusely

Lay with me and also with them

Spend quality time with me but give your heart to another

Feed me, mentally, physically, emotionally...and detach your emotions

I'll allow it all because all I know is hurt.

The concept of having a lover that is completely mine is foreign to me.

My curse to share.

I'd rather hurt myself

Alone

When the smoke clears
Before the words dry
You'll know that you're still alone

I don't know how many

It doesn't matter how many words or tokens of love are spoken to her

You'll still feel alone, even in her presence

Her disconnect, lack of respect

She can't handle your heart

She can't give you her word, you know it's more that you deserve

You'll still want her, need her, desire her

Open your heart to allow true love in

Open your mind to allow clarity and focus in but don't be a fool

To Me She Is

To me she is the sunrise. That warm glow you feel on your skin as the world wakes up. The smile that tugs on your heart when you hear a voice that comforts you. The purple, pinks, oranges and blue hues that show you magic is happening.

My comfort, my peace, my love. Leaving you is always hard. It always feels like a piece of my heart is missing. A piece of my heart is you.

I synchronize our breathing while you sleep to connect deeper. I ride the waves in the sea of your brown eyes. Lips sweet and soft reminding me of cotton candy, skin bright and glowing like shined pennies waiting to be spent. My love, your queen. So much potential for us both. So much love

To me who's is all of these things but she's stuck in a wave of what ifs.

Waste of time

You know that you deserve better but you choose to continue in the same merry go round

Love... to her a word without meaning. Concept gets lost when it's spread Ike mayo

Am I that desperate that I'm willing to accept what is given? I often find myself wondering why I bother.

What's the point of being a good woman ... loyal, faithful, subservient... if it can't be reciprocated, if it's not what they want.

I see the others ignore you yet you damn near beg for their attention. Only giving me 100% when you fear losing me.

You are losing me... do you even care? Do you understand?

I love you so simply, just for being you. You abuse that love, you dangle me on a string... a string I allow you to control as if you are the ultimate puppet master.

I'm tired of being a puppet I'm tired of being broken and left to put the pieces back together. My road, my journey of healing took too long for me to backslide

You give too much of yourself because you never learned how to give less. Always wanting to be a part of something... always wanting to be loved.

Pushing people away that are good for you yet the heartbreaker you embrace attesting that you can 'fix' them.

You know she doesn't love you. You are merely a convenience... a get away from the norm... a refreshing distraction.

But it's not love... it's a waste of time

Soon baby...

Titties throbbing
Pussy throbbing
I need to feel your mouth on me
I need to feel you touching me
I love when you grab my thighs
When you hold my pussy open and suck on my clit
When you kiss my back when we cuddle
When you choke me when I ride your face

Soon is not fast enough when I want you. The way my body feels... I can't even explain it. I want to come undone, I want to submit, I want to trust you with me... with my wants, with my desires.

I can tell that pleasuring me excites you so I want to make sure you are satisfied. I can hear and smell how wet you are while you feast on me. I moan in anticipation of what I know is coming.

I've waited so long for this...

As I stare into your eyes I know that what I feel is real. I've waited so long for this moment and now that I finally have you... covet

Love

Not words, actions, feelings ... emotions.

Taking care of your person from an emotional and physical aspect... fulfilled in ways other than physical.

Putting me 1st when I'm used to being an afterthought.

You confuse me. I'm not used to... wait, I know this pattern and I know what happens, torn between two.

What we have dissipates unbeknownst to you.

No more smiles or words of endearment.

No I love you's or affection, lack of attention due to your discretion.

Mood swings, shifty beings, spirit unaligned, too much pride and truth to deny.

Refuse to share or if I do I'll ever care.

You become a toy, a playmate, a series of dates... let me go

No Longer Asleep

As I lie here and watch you sleep I contemplate my own selfishness.

My need for you at this moment is strong but your need for sleep is stronger.

I fantasize and wish that you were awake... awake to kiss me, hold me and caress me as only you can.

You smile in your sleep and I smile to myself wondering what things could bring about such a sexy smile in your mind.

As if reading my thoughts you reach for me.

I moan in response as your hands lightly graze already hardened nipples.

Liking my response you reposition yourself to have more access.

No longer asleep, I contemplate my own selfishness, knowing you have to be up in a few hours, knowing that if we start this it will take a few hours.

You sigh in appreciation as you touch my most sensitive spot and find it wet to your liking.

Pull me in close to kiss you, hold me tightly as you inhale my scent.

As you bring me closer to no control I languidly close my eyes and yours begin to open.

No longer asleep, I question my own selfishness because my need is strong.

You put me over the edge and sleep is inevitable.

I glance at the clock and see that my selfishness has made you late for your daily routine.

I succumb to sleep as only an insomniac could as you are wide awake, satisfied and unselfish with your love for me...

No longer asleep

Lazy

I giggled as I came all over her face.

Chin dripping with my juice, body totally relaxed.

She removed her fingers from both of my now super sensitive holes and began kissing my inner thighs.

I tried to roll off of her eager mouth but she held my hips in place, gently licking my clit and starting yet another slow grind on her face.

She squeezed my ass with a firm but gentle grip as I bounced lightly on her thick, long tongue. Reaching up she pulled at my nipples, catching the piercings between her fingers. She tugged, I moaned; she pinched, I ground my pussy deeper into her face. She sighed as I began to drip sweet pussy juice in her mouth. Never missing a beat, she alternated between licks and sucking, from the back all the way to the tip. I felt my body tense up preparing for release. I began arching my back and rubbing my nipples as the pressure from her tongue increased.

I began moaning and stuttering out her name. Head whipping side to side, I bit my lip and she latched onto my thighs and pulled me deep onto her tongue. It started in my toes as she did slow circles in my opening coaxing out the cum. I giggled again signaling I was almost there. She reached up and grabbed my hair causing me to arch back, shoulders on her raised knees.

She gently bit my clit 4 times whispering "Cum for me Baby" MmmMmmhhhhmm was all i could muster. Body on fire, I whimpered as I felt my orgasm getting closer. She released my hair and began massaging my ass, slowly working her middle finger in. Once she got pass the tight opening she began pumping slowly. I'm cummming...ohhhh baby I moaned.

My clit got hotter and hotter, my natural response was to bounce faster and grind my pussy on her mouth harder and faster. OH SHIIIIITTTT BABY!!! I felt, and heard a gush as I squirted all over her face.

Neck, chin, ears and cheeks dripping with cum. Baby kissed me one last time as I collapsed face first on the bed. She smacked me on the ass and called me lazy as I fell asleep with a smile on my face

Talk yo' Shit

She smiled flirtatiously knowing I would give her exactly what she wanted. I gripped the back of her neck. Not enough to hurt, but with enough pressure for her to know I was serious.

Tell me what you want, I whispered against her lips. She visibly trembled and whimpered her response. I gripped just a bit harder and stepped closer. TELL ME ... she looked me in my eyes and said simply... you.

Her reward for obedience will be just that... a taste of me. I slowly run my hands through her locs, massing her scalp. She moaned in pleasure. As her back arched, neck exposed, I leaned in for a quick taste. Gently biting her neck, shoulder, wherever I could quickly get my mouth. She stiffened and then groaned. I knew what that meant, my baby came for me.

I supported her back while reaching down to caress her trembling thighs. She gripped my wrist and I quickly backed away. She knows not to touch me yet. I question her with my eyes and let them travel down her body. Damn... I can see the cum seeping out of her pussy onto her thighs. I need to taste her now.

I remind myself of all the written words, unspoken innuendo filled with desire ... basically all that shit talking thru text. I drop to my knees to properly worship the greatest place, feeling, taste embodiment of womanhood I've had the pleasure of being near.

I'm mesmerized by what's in front of me. I'm visibly watching her reaction to me. My mouth waters as I see her pussy get wetter and wetter. I run my finger from the top, past her piercing, between lips and enjoy the feeling of her plump pussy sucking me in.

I lean in for my first taste and am almost overwhelmed by the sensation it gives.

Does she know I'm addicted to her? That I can't breathe without her?

I grip her hips forcing her to widen her stance so I can have better access. I just ... gahdamn... I love eating pussy. I love eating HER pussy. I love the way her pussy reacts to me, I know I do that to her. I know she reserves this for me.

I start by sucking on her thighs making sure I lick up all her juices. We don't waste shit around here. I suck on the crease of her thigh which pleases me from her response. I can hear her pussy bubbling over. I drag my tongue very slowly from the base of her pussy several times. Stopping each time I feel she is going to cum. I continue to get more and more aroused from her excitement. I have to remind myself to go slow, to savor her.

I stop my assault on her pussy just to take a moment to simply gaze at her. She's so beautiful when she's about to cum. Eyes lazy, skin flushed, breathing labored. I could just eat and watch her cum all day.

She's getting antsy from lack of touch so I quickly get back to touching her anywhere my hands, fingers, lips, tongue can process. I love sucking on her neck and trailing kisses to her breasts. Licking around each nipple and then sucking on it with gentle bites in between.

I make sure to brush my fingers against her clit while paying attention to her breasts and stomach. Just rubbing up and down her pussy feeling her legs trembling. I slide one finger inside her and watch as she arches her back.

She attempted to push me away but my lips found hers and she relaxed. She trusts me. She feels amazing, so warm, so wet. I can feel my own orgasm building just from touching her intimately. I dip just a little lower and start kissing on her pussy while still fingering her slowly. I kiss down both lips and spread them slightly with my tongue.

Damn she's so wet. Licking and sucking on her clit causes me to lose control and as I cum I bite down softly on her which causes her to release as well. Damn she tastes so good. As her breathing returns to normal I Kiss my way back up her body still feeling her trembling under me. I kiss her lips, her chin, both cheeks and her forehead.

Words unspoken, she trusts me but is still scared. Now in bed I lay on her chest with fingers tangled in her locs listening to her heart beat as she fell asleep.

I want you to fuck me (Extended Session)

But ...

In order to open my pussy you have to learn how to open my mind. Days turn into weeks with you, conversations and intentions make us lose track of time. Melodic voices and murmurs in your ears as I hold you close. I want you. I want you to know how much.

How do I tell you I know how this ends? Will you comprehend that our children are beautiful and our wedding was simple just as we discussed. Can I tell you I love you devoid of words?

Time hovers over our heads with words left unsaid. It's too soon lingers between us like stale air ... but I don't want to lose you. Giving you opportunities to open me fully, to experience all of me. Baby I'm tired of holding back.

I love that you wake up thinking of me. Cerebral passages imprinted with my essence. Imprinted on your body they'd find me if they knew where to look... Amazing woman indeed, a spectacular influence you weren't aware you'd need. I offer myself to you if you give permission.

Open my mind so that I can properly open my body. I want you uninhibited with me. You can't fuck me like you did her or them ... it's ... different. It's always about your pleasure as I'm pleased to be of service. Submission to you for me is natural. I need it, I need you ... but ... all you hear is what I say ... I want you to fuck me ... damn

When you've given up on finding someone who completes you and resign yourself to just be content or dare I say settle ... life has a way of making things interesting. Not looking, searching, yearning for or even thinking about completing me... she has come in my life and given me a beautiful disruption.

What is a soul mate? Your equal? Someone you can't live without? Someone who shares moments, life experiences, who understands your hurts and listens to love you better. Is this love, well, not yet, but tracking.

When you have some who will act a fool over you and it's ok because you'd do the same ... that's dangerous. Been looking for reciprocity, found something that may be better. Found something that may last a little bit longer... speaking of last ...

Too fast... two days slowed us down...full speed... she said she missed me more... damn

We ain't quite a couple but we more than friends

Pt 2

Time, fate, perception and misconceptions will leave you confused and speaking things into existence that should never be. One sided feelings lead to not even dealing, but for clarity you just tryna be friends right?

I put my eggs in your basket, fool I am. I left my time at your will, shame on me. You can have your friend, just understand I don't blur lines. You still trying to fuck me?

Indecisiveness leads to my attention being less than what you desire ... Why are you afraid ? Emotions won't kill you... not having me won't either.

Don't worry, I won't change. I'll give you what you ask for and even what you don't. You need my love just as much as I need to give it to you... damn ... what the fuck are we doing
You'd be a fool to not take me as I am
Love is exhausting but I'm not tired of you yet

Pt 3

Need you

Want you

Feel me

React to you

Mine

Pt 4 the arrival, the breaking point

I see forever in her... I need her to see her potential. Am I caught up again in what could be? The promise of what is or am I still looking for a replacement. She's unlike the others. Walk, talk, affect aligns with me. When the cravings begin ... she handled me like a lover who's known you for ages. This is some past life shit neither of us are prepared for.

Pt 5 the unexpected

Cravings ... you.

Pt 6 The change up

What wasn't to be expected affected what was being built. Words said out of anger cause ripples in straight lines. I can't build with unresolved trauma. I told you I just wanted to fuck.

Pt 7 lacking…

Interest and attraction are a funny thing ... I can be both at the same time or neither in the same place. Cliche but my cutoff game is strong. You fell in love, it's one sided but now I'm wrong? I put myself 1st, not entertaining the drama. My shit doesn't come with baggage and I won't allow you to mismanage me

Pt 8 the chase or whatever the fuck this was

you should have just fucked me and left me alone

EGO

Jumbled thoughts and words occupy headspace already occupied by you. Protection spells float with white light and divinity over your head. Prayers for you, over you, surround you. My sunshine, my warmth, my light, my peace in a chaotic space.

Your smile when it doesn't reach your eyes breaks my heart. I never want to hurt you. I'd give you a million reasons to smile daily if able.   I wish I could bottle you up and sprinkle you around me. Your soul is peace
and tranquility and warmth and fire and love and ... damn. Unaware of how dope you are, an addiction I wouldn't mind shooting through my veins.

Unassuming and lacking ego, driven by your own beat. Naive to the beauty that is you. I could stare at you for hours and find different ways to admire your beauty. It's in the way you walk, the confidence in your step, the shyness in your speech, the explosion in your passion, the softness of your moans. Every part of you working together for what is perfectly impressive & lacking nothing

When I tell you I love you

I feel like you're ready, these 3 words are something you need to hear. A weight off my shoulders, I only speak intention to those I hold near

A love without strings or contingency ... a love that has filtered thru me first. Not looking for you to complete me or reciprocate what I feel. Love is happy, love is free, love is what I exude to those around me. It's hard not to feel loved in my presence. It's hard not to love you for all that you are. Perfectly imperfect, the missing piece to the puzzle I never intended to start. Time stopper, charmer, woman of many talents... you deserve love.

You don't get told enough that you are loved. "Women glow differently when they are loved properly" allow me to assist you. Allow the light from my love to cover you, encompass you, devour you, enjoy you, yet love you so sweet and gentle.

Love is multidimensional, I'm not confused with my intent. If your smile makes me happy
-I love that part of you

Engaging in conversation that leaves me stimulated
-I love that part of you

Your insecurities that you are comfortable sharing with me
-I love that part of you

Your fucking heart and how it mirrors my need to help others -I love that part of you

When I tell you I love you, feel that shit in your toes, let it run up your thighs, touch your most sensitive places, caress your breasts, kiss your neck, whisper in your ear and land on your lips.

I love you for what you are, what I see when I look at you, and your acceptance of me without any pretense, the best version of me loves this version of you.

Balance

She knows that I need control but I always give her balance. Her femininity disguised by her masculine appearance blends perfectly with my unassuming aggression that lies beneath the surface. On the outside they see me ... well what I want them to see. She looks deeper, further... she sees the ability to relinquish control in me. I provide a safe space for her to not be what society thinks she is. An outlet if you will.

She gives and I take, we repeat and then slow it down. My special place, home ... when she says it has a deeper meaning. No longer where the heart is, home is me and she knows she can always come to it. A safe haven, peace, expression, creativity. Unashamed in my desire for her I can literally breathe in her exhales. When she touches me ...

When she touches me I feel whole. I feel ... electric current, passion I can't even comprehend, the sweetest kisses with your hand around my throat. Gladly I gave her control... tired of being strong, wanting to serve, wanting to be wanted.

Understanding her need for dominance and letting her have her way is my control. Her eyes, her lips and her hands take possession of me. I allow it with no uncertainty... I trust her, she balances me. Wanting to protect her as she fights for me. Wanting to soothe her when her mind is uneasy. Feeding her ego with affirmation and love I watch her bloom like flowers waiting for the first peek of spring.

I see the change in me from loving her. No longer tipping the scales. No longer building a wall. No longer the aggressive... She is my balance.

Stubborn

Unwilling
Unyielding
Uninterested

The constant push and pull, exchange of power and emotion. Both stubborn, only one willing to relinquish control.

Only one willing to make it right. I push and push some more until it becomes a chase as you pull away.

Just wanting you close to me unable to bring you close to me.
Affection-less affection is what you desire.

Only on your terms, only at your request ... only ... that doesn't work for me.

My desire, need and craving to be near any part of you is too strong.

My want to ingest you is too strong for you. My need is too strong for you.

Too stubborn to give into desire, to stubborn to allow release of full emotion, too stubborn to relinquish control.

With you I want different but you remain the same, closed out of fear or hurt, you won't open up.
I see your vulnerability and then just as quick it's hidden again.

Double Penetration

Mind and heart

Heal me from hurts no one has ever apologized for ...

The End

I told you this wasn't a Love Story! Thank you! Thank you! This is my baby, my first work and I hope that it is not my last. A labor of love indeed. This art is 20 years in the making… chronicling my first heartbreak, opening up myself to love again, heartbreak again, infidelities, and LOVE.

I hope that you read this book, saw a little bit of yourself in it and decided that you wanted to do the work to produce better outcomes. I hope my journey has inspired you to open yourself back up to love. I want your reluctance and trust issues to dissipate as you realize that not all men and women are created the same. I hope to be the friend in your head when you are contemplating your situation. The one who tells you that you are more than enough and that you can do way better than what you are.

I would love it if you reached out to me or left a review
Instagram: @taetheremix

Made in the USA
Columbia, SC
28 June 2022

62403737R00043